YEARS 3 AND 4

Teacher's Moderation Toolkit

BOOK

2

Standardisation Resource for Writing

Prim-Ed
Publishing

Teacher's Moderation Toolkit *(Book 2)*

Published by Prim-Ed Publishing® 2017
Copyright© St Helens Teaching School Alliance® 2017

ISBN 978-1-84654-883-3

6657PR

Titles available in this series:

Teacher's Moderation Toolkit *(Book 1)*
Teacher's Moderation Toolkit *(Book 2)*
Teacher's Moderation Toolkit *(Book 3)*

Internet Websites

In some cases, websites or specific URLs may be recommended. While these are checked and rechecked at the time of publication, the publisher has no control over any subsequent changes which may be made to webpages. It is *strongly* recommended that the class teacher checks *all* URLs before allowing pupils to access them.

View all pages online

Website: http://www.prim-ed.com

Email: sales@prim-ed.com

Ensuring accurate teacher assessment of writing and consistency across school is high on the agenda for many primary school teachers. The *Teacher's Moderation Toolkit* provides everything that is needed to equip staff with a range of resources to:

- support their own judgements, by providing high-quality, standardised, termly examples of real children's writing;

- provide staff with examples of writing that they can annotate in phases or clusters, using non-negotiable writing sheets referenced to the national curriculum, which can be checked against annotated examples in the resource book; and

- share exemplars with pupils, to raise expectations, to peer assess a neutral piece of writing and to up-level writing.

Contents

Acknowledgements
for Teacher's Moderation Toolkit

Maddy Barnes – **Editor**

St Helens Teaching School Alliance

St Mary and St Thomas' CE Primary School

Chorley New Road Primary School

St Ann's CE Primary School

St Theresa's Catholic Primary School

Queen's Park Primary School

The District CE Primary School

Rectory CE Primary School

Robins Lane Primary School

Willow Tree Primary School

Sutton Oak Primary School

Chapel End Primary School

Eccleston Lane Ends Primary School

Holy Cross Catholic Primary School

Rivington Primary School

Broad Oak Primary School

St Thomas of Canterbury Catholic Primary School

Sutton Manor Primary School

Corpus Christi Catholic Primary School

St Mary's Catholic Federation

Newton Le Willows Primary School

Spinney Avenue Primary School

Thatto Heath Primary School

Legh Vale Primary School

The following people need a special mention:

Dawn Robertson
English Consultant

Mick Robertson
Artist

Shareen Mayers
English Advisor

SLEs (Specialist Leaders in Education) that have helped to write, edit and QA the resource:

Huw Foulkes Jones
St Theresa's Catholic Primary School

Michelle Slingsby
St Mary and St Thomas' CE Primary School
(part of the Three-Saints Academy Trust)

Laura Rynn
St Ann's CE Primary School
(part of the Three-Saints Academy Trust)

Ruth McKenny
Rivington Primary School

Nicola Rutter
St Silas CE Primary School
(part of the Rainbow Trust)

The **Teacher's Moderation Toolkit** is a three-book series that can be used in a variety of ways to support accurate teacher assessment of writing for years 1 to 6. It can be used to standardise and benchmark children's writing at three termly intervals, as a CPD resource to support teachers working together to make judgements and also as a classroom resource to share the expected standards of writing with children.

An experienced team of moderators, consultants, SLEs and teachers have worked together to compile a moderation toolkit using real children's writing.

Currently, writing is teacher assessed at both Key Stage 1 and Key Stage 2. Teachers are expected to assess a collection of children's writing that illustrate writing for different purposes and in different forms; for example, a child may write a persuasive letter, an informative leaflet, a story with a flashback, a narrative poem and a survival guide linked to their creative curriculum. Assessing a collection of writing requires teachers to be able to identify features in the child's writing, answering the questions:

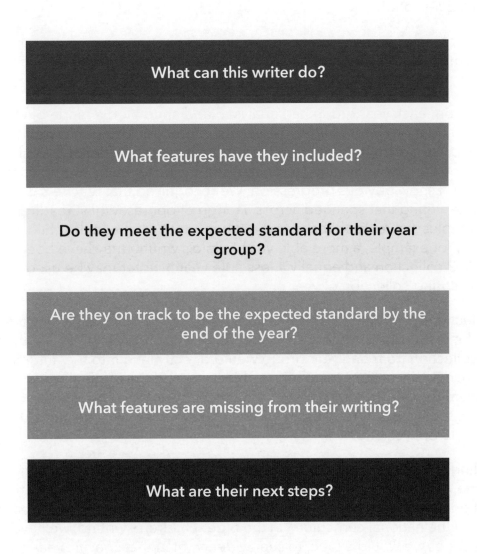

What can this writer do?

What features have they included?

Do they meet the expected standard for their year group?

Are they on track to be the expected standard by the end of the year?

What features are missing from their writing?

What are their next steps?

Methodology
used when Creating this Toolkit

Many schools have worked together to create writing portfolios of what is the expected standard for each year group. As a teaching school alliance, we recognised that teachers would benefit from a moderated, standardised toolkit that could both assist and guide teachers when making termly judgements about children's writing.

Initially, we worked with English subject leaders spanning a range of local authorities in the north-west of England. Schools were given a set of writing tasks to complete with years 1–6 so that it would be easier to make comparisons when moderating the writing.

The first task was a picture prompt of a girl called Lizzie in a silver birch tree (See Appendix A) and children were asked to write a description. The following term, schools were given a choice of writing prompts related to other pictures of Lizzie – a newspaper report, a narrative and a diary.

As schools collated evidence of children writing at different points in the year, we decided to offer specific year group moderating sessions where teachers brought samples of children's writing and annotated them in groups (some of these samples feature as part of the resource). At this point teachers did not use any criteria to moderate with. Instead they focused on the question:

What can this writer do? and annotated the writing with appropriate labels; for example, noun phrases, multi-clause sentences, range of tenses, use of direct speech, commas in a list etc.

After teachers from each year group had analysed and annotated a range of writing, English subject leaders and moderators began the selection process. Using the writing objectives for each year group, we began to make decisions about what the evidence files should look like. We were very keen for the collections to be realistic, include writing examples that teachers see every day and show obvious progression. We recognised that teachers would want to see examples of writing that spanned across a range of genres. Whilst reading through the annotated examples, we realised that it was not important what age the child who wrote the writing was; for example, a more able year 1 child's writing may have been used in the autumn of year 2 collection and equally a less able year 5 writer may be used as a good example in the spring collection of year 4.

Once the collections of writing had been established, a group of SLEs and moderators worked with the resource. Our priority was that there was progression within the toolkit and the summer collection from one year group would directly lead into the autumn collection of the next. Once again, national curriculum objectives and the original work samples in Appendix B were regularly referred to and referenced to ensure consistency. Final decisions were made, the toolkit was agreed upon and resulted in 3 termly collections of writing for each year group from year 1 to 6.

All of the writing examples have been typed up verbatim for ease and are annotated with some of the main features expected for specific year groups; for example, writing in the year 1 collection is annotated with features teachers would expect to see in year 1 writing, as prescribed in the national curriculum. In the older children's writing, we have again focused on features we would expect to see evidence of in that specific year group and not commented on every single feature included by the child.

Annotated version of the collections of children's writing.

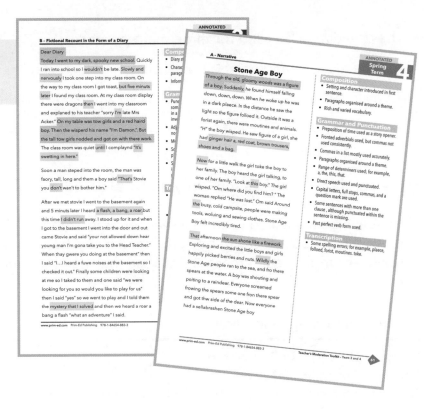

Unannotated versions of the collections of children's writing.

Writing non-negotiable grids per year group to use when assessing writing.

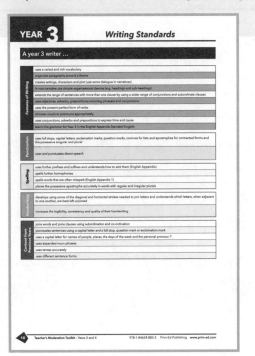

How to Use
the Teacher's Moderation Toolkit

The toolkit can be used for three main purposes:

- as a termly standardised benchmark for teachers;

- as a CPD resource for teachers to use when moderating; and

- as a classroom teaching resource to share with pupils.

How can it be used as a termly standardised benchmark for teachers?

Most teachers are asked to submit teacher assessment of writing on a termly basis. Teachers can use the collection of writing in the toolkit as a benchmark to compare their children with; for example, Year 4 teachers can use the Year 4 autumn collection in the autumn term (December).

If the child being assessed is:

writing **broadly in line** with the writing in the collection	the child is writing at the expected standard.
writing at **a higher standard** than the writing in the collection	the teacher should refer to the next term and confirm that the child is writing at greater depth.
not writing at the standard of the writing in the collection	the teacher should refer to the collection for the previous term and confirm that the child is writing at below the expected standard.

Teachers may want to look at the collection of writing for their year group and complete a similar task with their class; for example, in the autumn of year 3 the collection of writing consists of:

1. *Non-chronological report*
2. *Fictional recount in the form of a diary*
3. *Recount*
4. *Description*
5. *Explanation*

Completing a similar task with your children can make the benchmarking process even more straightforward.

How can it be used as a CPD resource for teachers to use when moderating?

Ensuring that the teacher assessment of writing is accurate is a whole school responsibility and one of the most pivotal forms of CPD in relation to this is completing whole school moderations, phase moderations or clusters of moderations. In order to be completely neutral, it can be more beneficial for teachers to use writing from children unknown to them. When teachers use their own children's writing for moderation purposes, it can be difficult to remain neutral and teachers can be tempted to give children the benefit of the doubt rather than assess what is there in the evidence.

The moderation toolkit provides teachers with collections of children's writing to assess. Schools can arrange opportunities in staff meetings for teachers to assess the writing from the toolkit. Teachers can use the unannotated versions and identify features in the child's writing by referring to the writing non-negotiable sheets. Then teachers can work together to annotate the writing. Once completed, teachers can then compare their annotated versions with the annotated versions in the toolkit. This process highlights the importance of using a criteria and analysing writing to identify evidence. Using the non-negotiable sheets will assist teachers in becoming more fluent with the expectations for their year group. Completing tasks like this throughout the academic year will ensure that teachers are confident, and more importantly accurate, when making their termly teacher assessments of writing.

How can it be used as a classroom teaching resource to share with pupils?

When teaching high quality writing lessons, it is important to share clear expectations with children. This can be presented in various forms – through success criteria, learning ladders, peer assessment etc. However, one of the most powerful forms is through sharing a piece of writing that a child has written. Teachers can use the writing from the toolkit collection as an example for what they expect the children to produce. This can take place in a number of ways:

- Display an unannotated piece of writing and ask children to identify features of writing in the evidence. Teachers can then display the annotated version for children to compare. This is a good opportunity to consolidate learning and use key terminology with children.

- Display a piece of writing from the collection to read with children. Give children a hard copy of the writing and ask them to edit and improve the writing using what they know about their year group expectations. This can be used as evidence of children making choices and editing.

A year 3 writer ...

Features of Writing

uses a varied and rich vocabulary.
organises paragraphs around a theme.
creates settings, characters and plot in narratives.
In non-narrative use simple organisational devices (e.g. headings and sub-headings).
extends the range of sentences with more than one clause by using a wider range of conjunctions and subordinate clauses.
uses adjectives, adverbs, prepositions (including phrases) and conjunctions.
uses the present perfect form of verbs.
chooses nouns or pronouns appropriately.
uses conjunctions, adverbs and prepositions to express time and cause.
learns the grammar for Year 3 in the English Appendix Standard English.

Punctuation

uses full stops, capital letters, exclamation marks, question marks, commas for lists and apostrophes for contracted forms and the possessive singular and plural.
uses and punctuates direct speech.

Spelling

uses further prefixes and suffixes and understands how to add them (English Appendix).
spells further homophones.
spells words that are often misspelt (English Appendix 1).
places the possessive apostrophe accurately in words with regular and irregular plurals.

Handwriting

develops using some of the diagonal and horizontal strokes needed to join letters and understands which letters, when adjacent to one another, are best left unjoined.
increases the legibility, consistency and quality of their handwriting.

Content from Previous Years

joins words and joins clauses using subordination and co-ordination.
punctuates sentences using a capital letter and a full stop, question mark or exclamation mark.
uses a capital letter for names of people, places, the days of the week and the personal pronoun 'I'.
uses expanded noun phrases.
uses tenses accurately.
uses different sentence forms.

Genre of Samples:

A: Non-Chronological Report

B: Fictional Recount in the Form of a Diary

C: Recount

D: Description

E: Explanation

Rocks

Introduction

Have you ever wondered about the pebble in your pocket? This report is about interesting rocks.

Types of rocks

Rocks can have different names like obsidian, granite and even chalk to.

Rocks can be used for things like houses, streets and even stairs.

Where rocks are found

Rocks can be in different places and some can be found in firey volcanoes.

How rocks are made

Igneous rocks are formed when magma from volcanoes slowly cools down and turns solid. other rocks are made from other little pieces under the lake and washes.

Composition

- Simple organisational devices; for example, headings and subheadings used.
- Paragraphs are mostly under relevant headings.
- Formal style appropriate for report.

Grammar and Punctuation

- Appropriate tenses.
- Most sentences correctly demarcated, including commas in a list and a question mark.
- Correct use of adverbs and adjectives to create noun phrases.

Transcription

- Most spelling is correct, including some technical vocabulary.

B – Fictional Recount in the Form of a Diary

Dear Diary

Today I went to my dark, spooky new school. Quickly I ran into school so I wouldn't be late. Slowly and nervously I took one step into my class room. On the way to my class room I got toast, but five minuts later I found my class room. At my class room display there were dragons then I went into my classroom and explaned to his teacher "sorry I'm late Mrs Acker." On my table was tow girls and a red haird boy. Then the wisperd his name "I'm Damon,". But the tall tow girls nodded and got on with there work. The class room was quiet until I complaynd "It's swetting in here."

Soon a man steped into the room, the man was faory, tall, long and them a boy said "That's Stovie you don't wan't to bother him."

After we met stovie I went to the basement again and 5 minuts later I heard a flash, a bang, a roar, but this time I didn't run away. I stood up for it and when I got to the basement I went into the door and out came Stovie and said "your not allowed down hear young man I'm gona take you to the Head Teacher." When thay gwere you doing at the basement" then I said "I...I heard a fuwe noises at the basement so I checked it out." Finally some children were looking at me so I taked to them and one said "we were looking for you so would you like to play for us" then I said "yes" so we went to play and I told them the mystery that I solved and then we heard a roar a bang a flash "what an adventure" I said.

Composition

- Diary starts by describing the setting.
- Characters introduced in first paragraph.
- Informal style appropriate for diary.

Grammar and Punctuation

- Punctuation mostly accurate, including some contractions and commas in a list. There is an attempt to use inverted commas.
- Adjectives used to create expanded noun phrases.
- Mostly appropriate tenses.
- Some use of adverbials, prepositional phrases and conjunctions.
- Some cohesive devices to organise ideas – beginning to paragraph, pronouns and dialogue.

Transcription

- Some spelling is correct, although many errors; for example, minuts, tow, there, thay.
- Errors with past tense 'ed'; for example, wisperd, complaynd, steped.

On Thursday 10th March Class 3/4 went to Saint Matthews Church bootle. We went because it was part of are topic work. We went to find out what happens in a church and what they use things in the church.

First Mrs Stanford split us into two groups and I was in the first group I went on the minibus and when I arrived at the Church we went into a room and played some games. the games were colded copy cat, shortest to big and we did all off are birthday and she gave us some informationabout Saint Matthews church. Mrs Stanford is a very good

Next we went into the big, cold church and explord it first I saw the brown wodden cross. Next I saw the font they use the font to crisen babys. Then I saw the alters. Then I saw the beautiful, big and colourful stain glass windows. Then I saw the numbers they were told what they were going to sing or what they are going to read in the bible. Then I saw lectern was to hold the bibble Then I saw the pulpit was used for the vicar to stand to welcome the congeration.

Sophie and Masie did a reading from the bibble and wecongeration. Then we betendid to be the chroir and we sung deep down inside. Then we asked kate so some questions. That the spire points to heven.

Finally before the first group went we had a biscat. The first group went back on the minibus and went back to school with Mrs Stanfords clever driving. The Best part of my day was when I was the choir.

Composition
- Adverbs used to help paragraph organisation.
- Mostly factual writing style suited to recounting the events.

Grammar and Punctuation
- Appropriate tenses.
- Some use of conjunctions (co-ordinating and subordinating).
- Adverbs used as a cohesive device alongside some attempt to paragraph.
- Adjectives used to create expanded noun phrases.

Transcription
- Some spelling is correct, although there are errors; for example, biscat, betendid, explord, crisen.

The T-Rex is a type of dinosaur which is now extinct. Would you know a dinosaur if you saw one? They have a long, curly, swishy tail and tiny little arms. Nearly all of them are colured in red. However sine are spikly than a hedgehog. And they are muddy brown to hide behind the trees.

A T-Rex live in Broadoak. Also they like to sleep on the mobiles. Most of them like going asemmbleys. How loud it is!

A T-Rex hunts for dinner ladys. Their favioreive meal is teachers and chips. Additionally they use a sharp, pointy pencil to clean his teeth.

These dinosaurs like to play football outside. However they can be clumpsy and hit the ball at you so be careful you have been warned.

Finally the most amazing thing about them is they sing really loudly and wake up the whole world.

Composition

- Adverbs used to build a range of sentence structures.
- Descriptive writing style, with use of adjectives, suited to the purpose of the text.

Grammar and Punctuation

- Most sentences correctly demarcated, including a question mark, exclamation mark and commas in a list.
- Appropriate tenses.
- Adjectives used for description.
- More challenging conjunctions; for example, However, Additionally.

Transcription

- Most spelling is correct, including some beyond the year 3 curriculum. Some errors in words; for example, colured, spikly, asemmbleys.

How do caterpillars grow?

Let me tell you how caterpillars grow. Stay and listen, its going to be interesting.

First, a butterfly lays an egg. the female butterfly normally leaves the egg on leaves or stems of plants.

The caterpillar grows inside the egg then it hatches and pops out. The caterpillar eats its way out of the egg and when it starts to chomp on leaves and host plants.

When then the catchrysalis. They normally do it on twigs or somewhere safe.

Once the butterfly is ready to come the puba splits open. But the butterfly still isn't ready yet the wings

Composition

- Writing style suited to purpose of an explanation text.
- Paragraphs organised around a theme; i.e. each paragraph explains a different stage in the life cycle of a butterfly.

Grammar and Punctuation

- Appropriate tenses.
- Adverbials used as cohesive devices.
- Some attempt to create multi-clause sentences.

Transcription

- Most spelling is correct. Child is using scientific language correctly, but with some spelling errors.

Genre of Samples:

A: Non-Chronological Report

B: Fictional Recount in the Form of a Diary

C: Recount

D: Description

E: Explanation

Rocks

Introduction

Have you ever wondered about the pebble in your pocket? This report is about interesting rocks.

Types of rocks

Rocks can have different names like obsidian, granite and even chalk to.

Rocks can be used for things like houses, streets and even stairs.

Where rocks are found

Rocks can be in different places and some can be found in firey volcanoes.

How rocks are made

Igneous rocks are formed when magma from volcanoes slowly cools down and turns solid. other rocks are made from other little pieces under the lake and washes.

B – Fictional Recount in the Form of a Diary

Dear Diary

Today I went to my dark, spooky new school. Quickly I ran into school so I wouldn't be late. Slowly and nervously I took one step into my class room. On the way to my class room I got toast, but five minuts later I found my class room. At my class room display there were dragons then I went into my classroom and explaned to his teacher "sorry I'm late Mrs Acker." On my table was tow girls and a red haird boy. Then the wisperd his name "I'm Damon,". But the tall tow girls nodded and got on with there work. The class room was quiet until I complaynd "It's swetting in here."

Soon a man steped into the room, the man was faory, tall, long and them a boy said "That's Stovie you don't wan't to bother him."

After we met stovie I went to the basement again and 5 minuts later I heard a flash, a bang, a roar,but this time I didn't run away. I stood up for it and when I got to the basement I went into the door and out came Stovie and said "your not allowed down hear young man I'm gona take you to the Head Teacher." When thay gwere you doing at the basement" then I said "I…I heard a fuwe noises at the basement so I checked it out." Finally some children were looking at me so I taked to them and one said "we were looking for you so would you like to play for us" then I said "yes" so we went to play and I told them the mystery that I solved and then we heard a roar a bang a flash "what an adventure" I said.

On Thursday 10th March Class $\frac{3}{4}$ went to Saint Matthews Church bootle. We went because it was part of are topic work. We went to find out what happens in a church and what they use things in the church.

First Mrs Stanford split us into two groups and I was in the first group I went on the minibus and when I arrived at the Church we went into a room and played some games. the games were colded copy cat, shortest to big and we did all off are birthday and she gave us some informationabout Saint Matthews church. Mrs Stanford is a very good

Next we went into the big, cold church and explord it first I saw the brown wodden cross. Next I saw the font they use the font to crisen babys. Then I saw the alters. Then I saw the beautiful, big and colourful stain glass windows. Then I saw the numbers they were told what they were going to sing or what they are going to read in the bible. Then I saw lectern was to hold the bibble Then I saw the pulpit was used for the vicar to stand to welcome the congeration.

Sophie and Masie did a reading from the bibble and wecongeration. Then we betendid to be the chroir and we sung deep down inside. Then we asked kate so some questions. That the spire points to heven.

Finally before the first group went we had a biscat. The first group went back on the minibus and went back to school with Mrs Stanfords clever driving. The Best part of my day was when I was the choir.

D – Description

The T-Rex is a type of dinosaur which is now extinct. Would you know a dinosaur if you saw one? They have a long, curly, swishy tail and tiny little arms. Nearly all of them are colured in red. However sine are spikly than a hedgehog. And they are muddy brown to hide behind the trees.

A T-Rex live in Broadoak. Also they like to sleep on the mobiles. Most of them like going asemmbleys. How loud it is!

A T-Rex hunts for dinner ladys. Their favioreive meal is teachers and chips. Additionally they use a sharp, pointy pencil to clean his teeth.

These dinosaurs like to play football outside. However they can be clumpsy and hit the ball at you so be careful you have been warned.

Finally the most amazing thing about them is they sing really loudly and wake up the whole world.

How do caterpillars grow?

Let me tell you how caterpillars grow. Stay and listen, its going to be interesting.

First, a butterfly lays an egg. the female butterfly normally leaves the egg on leaves or stems of plants. The caterpillar grows inside the egg then it hatches and pops out. The caterpillar eats its way out of the egg and when it starts to chomp on leaves and host plants.

When then the catchrysalis. They normally do it on twigs or somewhere safe.

Once the butterfly is ready to come the puba splits open. But the butterfly still isn't ready yet the wings

Genre of Samples:

A: Narrative

B: Newspaper Report

C: Description

D: Narrative

E: Recount

Evie's Adventure

The lightning struck as the spooky, black trees waved, while the wind was howling. As Evie the robot, walked down the path, she saw a creepy castle.

Suddenly all the lights turned on, Evie was realy scared, because the tall, scratched doors, slowly creaked open.

A few moments later, Evie decided to slowly tiptoe through the door. As soon as she got into the castle she saw a friendly wich. Because Evie didn't have any friends, she asked the wich if she wanted to be Evie's friend. The wich said, yes.

The next day, Evie and the wich decided to go on holiday so they went to a relaxing island called the Caribbean island. when they got there they was so relaxed.

Composition

- Setting and main character introduced in first paragraph.
- Rich vocabulary used for description.
- Adverbs used to help paragraph organisation.

Grammar and Punctuation

- Adjectives to create expanded noun phrases.
- Appropriate tenses.
- Some attempt to create multi-clause sentences.
- Some attempt to create multi-clause sentences using subordination/ adverbials.
- Punctuation mostly accurate, including apostrophes for contraction and possession. There is no attempt to punctuate direct speech.

Transcription

- Spelling mostly correct, with only a few spelling errors; for example, realy, wich.

Egg-salent arrival at broadoak school!

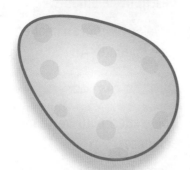

The egg is seventy-four centimetres (74 cm)

This morning at approximately 7am an unidentified egg was found in the blue gozebo by Mr Selfrichge. Maybe it was left there because the eggs mum thought it would be safe in a school.

Our reporter spoke to Summer (A pupil) who said "I have no clue where the cream egg came from or what is inside."

During the week children will be doing lessons based on the mystery egg. also when our reporter asked Olivia Witter (A pupil). She said "It is so egg-siting to find out what is in the egg. I think it will be a dragon."

A spokesperson for the Ministry for Mysterious Objects commented.

Composition

- Simple organisational devices used; for example, heading and caption.
- Factual style with interviews appropriate for a newspaper report.
- Paragraphs organised around a theme.

Grammar and Punctuation

- Tenses used are mostly accurate.
- Choosing vocabulary precisely to match the formality.
- Most sentences correctly demarcated, including inverted commas.
- Some attempt to create multi-clause sentences.

Transcription

- Most spelling is correct, including some challenging vocabulary for Year 3.

There was once a bird called cheecky who made everybody laugh and was very sneaky. He loved to joke with people and can sometime hurt people's feelings. Also lucky duckie was the youngest of all the birds and lucky duckie is alaways happy with what he can do. Lucky duckie was ra fly from tree to tree. The birds are all friends so they play like true friends.

All of the birds loved to play together and all loved to sleep. They are always flying in big groups and their wings are massive, that's how you can tell who is who. When it is raining or in winter all the birds hide in their nests away from the cold or rain. Sometimes people cut down their trees, so they have to find a new tree and make another nest. The birds need a home to survive and that's why people shouldn't cut down trees or destroy nature, because it hurts living things. They all built there nests by hand and it's hard because they only have little hands. Rainbow bird is very kind to other birds like Luckie duck

Composition

- Description has more narrative than descriptive elements.
- Developed from an image. (See Appendix A)

Grammar and Punctuation

- Some attempt to create multi-clause sentences.
- Tenses are mainly accurate.
- Subordinating and co-ordinating conjunctions used.
- Punctuation is mostly accurate – some correct use of the apostrophe.

Transcription

- Spelling mostly correct, with only a few spelling errors; for example, cheecky.

Once upon a time, there was a 11 year old boy called Super Spy Sam. And he has piercing blue eyes and platinum blonde hair and he loves going on adventures and that's why sam joined a super spy group. He also has a muscular body and rosy skin. He had a tall build and has long curly hair. Also he has dreams of hairdressers cutting his cute curls. He is also bold because he risks his life for others and he is brave. He is clean shaven.

Sam lived in a minischule, isolated village where nothing ever happened. In the centre there was a church with a spire on top. If you where to stand in the middle of the village you would hear the miserable moans of poor people getting frostbite on there fingers and there toes. Also sam's village was a sleepy village made out of shaken but look on the right side at least there is one gaugantuan school witch has a bit of heat but there looky because you don't get much heat on a mountainside. If you where to stand in the centre of the village you would smell wood cracking in the schorching, flamy fire.

Composition
- Main character introduced in first sentence.
- Detailed description of setting.
- Rich and varied vocabulary used.

Grammar and Punctuation
- Carefully chosen vocabulary to match the formaility–expanded noun phrases.
- Range of conjunctions used, including subordinating conjunctions.
- Some attempt to create multi-clause sentences.
- Prepositional phrases used.
- Punctuation is mostly accurate, including the apostrophe for possession.

Transcription
- Most spelling is correct, including some challenging vocabulary for Year 3.

Our trip to St Matthews

On Monday 7th March, class 3/4 SU went to St Matthew's Church to learn about Christianity because it is our RE topic.

First the class was split in half and one group went on the minibus with Miss Pendleton and the other half came later with Miss Sullivan. Mr Crilly drove the white, shiny minibus. I sat next to Joy, I felt excited.

Next the secend group did a church search wiul we wated for Mr Crilly to get us. We did the Church search in class. Then we went with Mr Crilly but some people never finesht there Church search and then we got on the minbus. Then we saw Kate, she toked to us for sixteen minutes. She told us when the Church was built in 1886. The roof was like he botem of a boat and the spire points to heaven.

After that Kate let us explore the Church properly. I saw a the woden purple hold kit, some bibles in the back of the church. Kate asked two people to read a short story to the rest of the children. Miss Sullivan choust Alex and Rayan, Alex was the reader and Rayan was the vicker. Also I saw the stand glass windows in the middil was Jesus and on the rite was Moses and we went back into the cominety room and had a bisket and a drink before we had to get back on the mini bus. The secend group played games wiul we wated for Mr Crilly.

Finally we went on the minibus. I had a really good time at St Matthew's Church and I will like to go back to St Matthew's Church and visit again. I really liked when Kate told us when the church was built.

Composition

- Recount retells events of a trip in chronological order.
- Informative style appropriate for the audience.
- Adverbs used to help paragraph organisation.

Grammar and Punctuation

- Punctuation is mostly accurate–although there is some incorrect use of the comma.
- Adverbials used as a cohesive device.
- Range of conjunctions used.
- Adjectives used to create expanded noun phrases.
- Tenses are mostly accurate.

Transcription

- Most spelling is correct. There are some errors with verb endings; for example, finesht, choust. There are also some errors with word endings; for example, vicker, middil, bisket.

Genre of Samples:

A: Narrative

B: Newspaper Report

C: Description

D: Narrative

E: Recount

Evie's Adventure

The lightning struck as the spooky, black trees waved, while the wind was howling. As Evie the robot, walked down the path, she saw a creepy castle.

Suddenly all the lights turned on, Evie was realy scared, because the tall, scratched doors, slowly creaked open.

A few moments later, Evie decided to slowly tiptoe through the door. As soon as she got into the castle she saw a friendly wich. Because Evie didn't have any friends, she asked the wich if she wanted to be Evie's friend. The wich said, yes.

The next day, Evie and the wich decided to go on holiday so they went to a relaxing island called the Caribbean island. when they got there they was so relaxed.

Egg-salent arrival at broadoak school!

This morning at approximately 7am an unidentified egg was found in the blue gozebo by Mr Selfrichge. Maybe it was left there because the eggs mum thought it would be safe in a school.

Our reporter spoke to Summer (A pupil) who said "I have no clue where the cream egg came from or what is inside."

During the week children will be doing lessons based on the mystery egg. also when our reporter asked Olivia Witter (A pupil). She said "It is so egg-siting to find out what is in the egg. I think it will be a dragon."

A spokesperson for the Ministry for Mysterious Objects commented.

C – Description

There was once a bird called cheecky who made everybody laugh and was very sneaky. He loved to joke with people and can sometime hurt people's feelings. Also lucky duckie was the youngest of all the birds and lucky duckie is alaways happy with what he can do. Lucky duckie was ra fly from tree to tree. The birds are all friends so they play like true friends.

All of the birds loved to play together and all loved to sleep. They are always flying in big groups and their wings are massive, that's how you can tell who is who. When it is raining or in winter all the birds hide in their nests away from the cold or rain. Sometimes people cut down their trees, so they have to find a new tree and make another nest. The birds need a home to survive and that's why people shouldn't cut down trees or destroy nature, because it hurts living things. They all built there nests by hand and it's hard because they only have little hands. Rainbow bird is very kind to other birds like Luckie duck

Once apon a time, there was a 11 year old boy called Super Spy Sam. And he has piercing blue eyes and platinum blonde hair and he loves going on adventures and that's why sam joined a super spy group. He also has a muscular body and rosy skin. He had a tall build and has long curly hair. Also he has dreams of hairdressers cutting his cute curls. He is also bold because he risks his life for others and he is brave. He is clean shaven.

Sam lived in a minischule, isolated village where nothing ever happened. In the centre there was a church with a spire on top. If you where to stand in the middle of the village you would hear the miserable moans of poor people getting frostbite on there fingers and there toes. Also sam's village was a sleepy village made out of shaken but look on the right side at least there is one gaugantuan school witch has a bit of heat but there looky because you don't get much heat on a mountainside. If you where to stand in the centre of the village you would smell wood cracking in the schorching, flamy fire.

Our trip to St Matthews

On Monday 7th March, class 3/4 SU went to St Matthew's Church to learn about Christianity because it is our RE topic.

First the class was split in half and one group went on the minibus with Miss Pendleton and the other half came later with Miss Sullivan. Mr Crilly drove the white, shiny minibus. I sat next to Joy, I felt excited.

Next the secend group did a church search wiul we wated for Mr Crilly to get us. We did the Church search in class. Then we went with Mr Crilly but some people never finesht there Church search and then we got on the minbus. Then we saw Kate, she toked to us for sixteen minutes. She told us when the Church was built in 1886. The roof was like he botem of a boat and the spire points to heaven.

After that Kate let us explore the Church properly. I saw a the woden purple hold kit, some bibles in the back of the church. Kate asked two people to read a short story to the rest of the children. Miss Sullivan choust Alex and Rayan, Alex was the reader and Rayan was the vicker. Also I saw the stand glass windows in the middil was Jesus and on the rite was Moses and we went back into the cominety room and had a bisket and a drink before we had to get back on the mini bus. The secend group played games wiul we wated for Mr Crilly.

Finally we went on the minibus. I had a really good time at St Matthew's Church and I will like to go back to St Matthew's Church and visit again. I really liked when Kate told us when the church was built.

Genre of Annotated Samples:

A: Report

B: Character Description

C: Newspaper Report

D: Newspaper Report

E: Diary

The Tongo Lizards back is scaly and spiky. It's belly is emerald green and lavar red. The Tongo Lizard 's eyes are shiny, bright and attractive. It's tail is as spiky as a knife. It's teeth are really spiky and sharp and as white as a pearl. It's claws are as sharp as scissors.

It lives in the wet, cold, gloomy, loud, noisy AMAZON rainforest. The trees are lime green and the branches are as brown as toffee. It lives in the trees and it makes its bed out of leaves.

It eats colourful flowers. And it's elergict to bird berries and bees. It also eats serten flies that are red and green. It's Endangered because people are building homes and they need to cut trees down.

Composition

- Paragraphs used to report on different aspects of the topic.
- Informative style appropriate for the audience.

Grammar and Punctuation

- Tenses are mostly accurate.
- Adjectives chosen to match the formality, including using similes.
- Punctuation is mostly accurate, including commas in a list and the apostrophe for contractions.

Transcription

- Most spelling is correct, including some challenging vocabulary for Year 3.

B – Character Description

The Big, Bad Robot was yellow, purple, red, blue and orange. His eyes were flashing red and green. He was as creacky as a rusty, old house. Also he has two shiney, golden stars on his front. The Big Bad Robit has two curly wirs on top of his head.

This mischievess character is very naughty indeed. He is never up to any good at all. I think he might be cross sometimes because everyone tells him what to do. He's very naughty and sometimes mischievous. Because he is very sneaky he is always in trouble. This naughty robot loves to play tricks on Winnie and Wilber.

This sneaky robots behaveure is bad because he pulled Winnie's nose and Wilber's tail so Winnie shouted at him! Because Winnie shouted at the robot he got even more bad. Everyone can assume that he wasn't very kind. He wasn't very kind because he stole Winnie's wand so she couldn't turn the robot back into a moddle.

Composition

- Description describes both the appearance and behaviour of the robot.

Grammar and Punctuation

- Tenses are mostly accurate.
- Punctuation is mostly accurate, including commas in a list and the apostrophe for contraction and possession.
- Adjectives are carefully chosen for effect.
- Subordination used as a cohesive device and writing is in paragraphs.

Transcription

- Most spelling is correct, including some challenging vocabulary for year 3.

The Daily Times

The world as gone "cuckoo"

Yesterday at approximately 1pm some extraordinary things happened …

Some of the peculiar sightings encluded over 100 sightings of owls across England. Our expert Lewis Sayers has said "This is very unusual for a Parliament of owls to fly during the day.' The owls have caused mayhem by sitting on telephone lines and sending the wrong messages to the police.

From Chester to Edinburgh, there have been reports that instead of rain it poured down shooting stars. Airports in particular are thinking that the shooting stars are planes. Around London people in cloaks are walking around in groups. These peculiar sightings have ___ across the UK. Many people seem to think that the shooting stars and the owls are caused by the mysterious people in cloaks. Others believe that there is dark magic in the air.

Composition

- Factual style with interview appropriate for a newspaper report.
- Paragraphs organised around a theme.

Grammar and Punctuation

- Tenses are mostly accurate.
- Precise language choices for formality.
- Development of multi-clause sentences.
- Punctuation is accurate, including good understanding of the capital letter for proper nouns.

Transcription

- Most spelling is correct, including spelling some challenging vocabulary for Year 3.

Groundshaking Disaster
THE DAILY MOON

During the tornado

On the 29.1.16 yesterday, a tornado striked into the village of Kings at 6am. Everyone was fast asleep when they herd a rumble and the ground shaking. Outside was an unbelievable sight, a gigantic tornado. The ground ripping and being flung into the tornado. People's bodies were smashing onto the floor with a big splat. The tornado was a level 10 and caused explosions.

As the emergency broadcast came off the TV, some people told it how it was, " 'orrible it was, me uncle died right in front of me eyes. Me 'ouse flung in the daft thing. Scary is was!" That was Tim Long's report. We also reported a woman called Victoria Lotsofdosh, "obviously it was frightening as of the emergency board."

Composition

- Simple organisational devices used; for example, heading and subheading.
- Factual style with interviews appropriate for a newspaper report.

Grammar and Punctuation

- Tenses are mostly accurate.
- Punctuation is mostly accurate, including an attempt to omit letters for dialect and apostrophes for possession.
- Challenging language choices to recount and create character.

Transcription

- Most spelling is correct, including some challenging vocabulary for Year 3.

Dear Diary

You won't believe what happened today! I was learning how to ride a two weeled bike until birds came in front of me! The birds started to flap their wings and peck my bike getting in the way so I could'nt see were I was going. As soon as the birds came my dad shouted as loud as he could to 'Be careful lizze my dear."

A few minutes after the birds were getting slow so I was able to peddle away. But then I realised I was on the road …

I started to shiver thinking what dad had said to me about being careful and looking were I was going. If it was'nt for those birds I would have been able to see, I also would'nt be on the road learning how to ride my bike. A few minutes later, I started to wobble on my bike the only reason for that was because I knew and felt I wasn't safe on the road. The road was so busy, long I couldn't turn of the huge, black road. I turned around and just about heard my dad shouting sayi" Come back but be careful" I then shouted back to dad "I need help coming of the road back home." Behind me I heard the sound of cars.

Then dad came rushing on was able to get me of the road in no time. Luckily enough I didn't get shouted a because it wasn't my fault it was the birds fault for pecking my bike and flapping their wings.

Composition

- Informal style appropriate for diary.
- Developed from an image. (See Appendix A.)

Grammar and Punctuation

- Tenses are mostly accurate.
- Punctuation is mostly accurate – inconsistent use of the apostrophe and inverted commas.
- Adverbials and conjunctions used as cohesive devices.
- Adjectives used to create expanded noun phrases.
- Language choices match the formality of story language.

Transcription

- Most spelling is correct. Child needs to be more secure when spelling using the apostrophe.

Genre of Samples:

A: Report

B: Character Description

C: Newspaper Report

D: Newspaper Report

E: Diary

A – Report

The Tongo Lizards back is scaly and spiky. It's belly is emerald green and lavar red. The Tongo Lizard 's eyes are shiny, bright and attractive. It's tail is as spiky as a knife. It's teeth are really spiky and sharp and as white as a pearl. It's claws are as sharp as scissors.

It lives in the wet, cold, gloomy, loud, noisy AMAZON rainforest. The trees are lime green and the branches are as brown as toffee. It lives in the trees and it makes its bed out of leaves.

It eats colourful flowers. And it's elergict to bird berries and bees. It also eats serten flies that are red and green. It's Endangered because people are building homes and they need to cut trees down.

B – Character Description

The Big, Bad Robot was yellow, purple, red, blue and orange. His eyes were flashing red and green. He was as creacky as a rusty, old house. Also he has two shiney, golden stars on his front. The Big Bad Robit has two curly wirs on top of his head.

This mischievess character is very naughty indeed. He is never up to any good at all. I think he might be cross sometimes because everyone tells him what to do. He's very naughty and sometimes mischievous. Because he is very sneaky he is always in trouble. This naughty robot loves to play tricks on Winnie and Wilber.

This sneaky robots behaveure is bad because he pulled Winnie's nose and Wilber's tail so Winnie shouted at him! Because Winnie shouted at the robot he got even more bad. Everyone can assume that he wasn't very kind. He wasn't very kind because he stole Winnie's wand so she couldn't turn the robot back into a moddle.

The Daily Times

The world as gone "cuckoo"

Yesterday at approximately 1pm some extraordinary things happened …

Some of the peculiar sightings encluded over 100 sightings of owls across England. Our expert Lewis Sayers has said "This is very unusual for a Parliament of owls to fly during the day.' The owls have caused mayhem by sitting on telephone lines and sending the wrong messages to the police.

From Chester to Edinburgh, there have been reports that instead of rain it poured down shooting stars. Airports in particular are thinking that the shooting stars are planes. Around London people in cloaks are walking around in groups. These peculiar sightings have ___ across the UK. Many people seem to think that the shooting stars and the owls are caused by the mysterious people in cloaks. Others believe that there is dark magic in the air.

Groundshaking Disaster
THE DAILY MOON

During the tornado

On the 29.1.16 yesterday, a tornado striked into the village of Kings at 6am. Everyone was fast asleep when they herd a rumble and the ground shaking. Outside was an unbelievable sight, a gigantic tornado. The ground ripping and being flung into the tornado. People's bodies were smashing onto the floor with a big splat. The tornado was a level 10 and caused explosions. As the emergency broadcast came off the TV, some people told it how it was, " 'orrible it was, me uncle died right in front of me eyes. Me 'ouse flung in the daft thing. Scary is was!" That was Tim Long's report. We also reported a woman called Victoria Lotsofdosh, "obviously it was frightening as of the emergency board."

Dear Diary

You won't believe what happened today! I was learning how to ride a two weeled bike until birds came in front of me! The birds started to flap their wings and peck my bike getting in the way so I could'nt see were I was going. As soon as the birds came my dad shouted as loud as he could to 'Be careful lizze my dear."

A few minutes after the birds were getting slow so I was able to peddle away. But then I realised I was on the road …

I started to shiver thinking what dad had said to me about being careful and looking were I was going. If it was'nt for those birds I would have been able to see, I also would'nt be on the road learning how to ride my bike. A few minutes later, I started to wobble on my bike the only reason for that was because I knew and felt I wasn't safe on the road. The road was so busy, long I couldn't turn of the huge, black road. I turned around and just about heard my dad shouting sayi" Come back but be careful" I then shouted back to dad "I need help coming of the road back home." Behind me I heard the sound of cars.

Then dad came rushing on was able to get me of the road in no time. Luckily enough I didn't get shouted a because it wasn't my fault it was the birds fault for pecking my bike and flapping their wings.

A year 4 writer ...

Features of Writing	
	uses a varied and rich vocabulary.
	organises paragraphs around a theme.
	creates settings, characters and plot in narratives.
	uses simple organisational devices (e.g. headings in non-narratives and subheadings).
	extends the range of sentences with more than one clause by using a wider range of conjunctions and subordinate clauses.
	use adjectives, adverbs, prepositions (including phrases) and conjunctions.
	uses the present perfect form of verbs.
	chooses nouns or pronouns appropriately.
	uses conjunctions, adverbs and prepositions to express time and cause.
	learns the grammar for Year 3 in the English Appendix Standard English.

Punctuation	
	uses full stops, capital letters, exclamation marks, question marks, commas for lists and apostrophes for contracted forms and the possessive singular and plural.
	uses and punctuates direct speech.

Spelling	
	uses further prefixes and suffixes and understands how to add them (English Appendix).
	spells further homophones.
	spells words that are often misspelt (English Appendix 1).
	places the possessive apostrophe accurately in words with regular and irregular plurals.

Handwriting	
	develops using some of the diagonal and horizontal strokes needed to join letters and understands which letters, when adjacent to one another, are best left unjoined.
	increases the legibility, consistency and quality of their handwriting.

Content from Previous Years	
	joins words and joins clauses using subordination and co-ordination.
	punctuates sentences using a capital letter and a full stop, question mark or exclamation mark.
	uses a capital letter for names of people, places, the days of the week and the personal pronoun 'I'.
	uses expanded noun phrases.
	uses tenses accurately.
	uses different sentence forms.
	uses direct speech.
	uses subordinate clauses.
	uses adjectives, adverbs, prepositions (including phrases) and conjunctions.

Genre of Samples:

A: Narrative

B: Description of a Scene

C: Diary

D: Newspaper

E: Report

A – Narrative

It was a cloudy afternoon and a small girl named Lizzie was sitting in the soft branches of her silver birch tree.

"Hallo" she wispered to the birds. "Are you okay today?" Chiff and Chaff answered politley "Yes" replied the twins. Suddenly the tree rocked violently. Egglet rolled off the tree an landed with a deafning thump! At the bottom of the tree stood Ghosyie, laughing his head off. Lizzie clambered down the tree. She examined the egg carefully. There was a gigantic crack through the top. When Lizzie went to rest for a nap Bananas and Snowy hooted at the tops of their voices. Magically Wizzling aooeared in a puff of threataning black smoke. With his magic crack was fixed. "Thank you" weezed the baby egg shyly. Postit flew past with a long brown envelope, dropping it in Lizzie's lap.

Dear Liz,

HELP! I'm stuck

Love Dad x

Lizzie dialed a number on her walkey-talkey 875 663. She spoke to him "Hi Dad" "Hi Lizzie" he said. She asked where he was stuck. "I'm stuck in a big ------ unfinished

Composition

- Setting and character introduced in first paragraph.
- Rich and varied vocabulary used.
- Developed from an image. (See Appendix A.)

Grammar and Punctuation

- Expanded noun phrases used.
- Appropriate nouns and pronouns.
- Direct speech is punctuated with inverted commas.
- Capital letters used for names of people and the personal pronoun 'I'.
- Adverbs and prepositions used to express time and cause.
- Full stops, capital letters, exclamation marks, question marks and apostrophes for contractions and singular possession.
- Fronted adverbials used, but without commas.
- Tenses used accurately.

Transcription

- Spelling mostly correct. Further understanding of suffixes needed; for example, -ly (politley), -en (deafn, threatan).

Anxiously, I edged towards the dark green forest. Below the trees stood a stick-like figure holding what looked like a dead animal. I saw a witch-like dwarf hiding in the trees, she was staring at the creature with its glowing red eyes. The tall, green trees, cut were swaying gently in a blow of the wind where in a deep, blue stream that went right through the forest. The tall, brown stick figure was marching through the deep, blue empty river he walked over to the bright, yellow light in the distance. Although the creature was splashing away, I saw the dwarf in the tree jump into the stream to chase him. Anxiously, I followed them to end my curiosity of them. The light was as bright as the sun, I knew that it was not the sun…

I got to the end of the forest, where were they

Composition

- Description has narrative and descriptive elements.
- Rich and varied vocabulary used.

Grammar and Punctuation

- Expanded noun phrases used.
- Beginnings of rich vocabulary; for example, stick-like figure.
- Capital letters, full stops and commas used.
- Appropriate nouns and pronouns.
- Subordination used; for example, Although.
- Adverbs and prepositions used; for example, gently, through.
- Commas used after fronted adverbials; for example, Anxiously.

Transcription

- Spelling mostly correct.

Dear Diary

Today I woke up tired and sleepy, but I still got up because it was my birthday! After that I ran past my dad and into the kitchen. Then I eat my breakfast realy quikly, after I eat my breakfast I ran back upstairs to get changed into my birthday cloths and I put my mum's make-up on just don't tell dad ok? Suddenly I heard a realy loud knock on my front door. I called my dad "Dad someone is knocking on the door" Then I slowly opend the door. "Hi Lizzie!" Tommy shouted. Then my dad said "I will bring the birthday cake in the minute" Then I jumped up and down whith exitment while I was blowing out the candles. Then the birthday candles went crazy! Luckly my dad ran in whith a bucket of water and he saved me and tommy.

Today was a dangrose day but a fun day to!

From Lizzie

Composition

- Informal style appropriate for diary.
- Developed from an image. (See Appendix A.)

Grammar and Punctuation

- Apostrophe used for possession and contracted forms.
- Tenses accurate, apart from eat/ate.
- Direct speech used and punctuated.
- Capital letters used for names of people and the personal pronoun 'I'.
- Coordination used; for example, but, while.
- Direct speech passes between present and future tense.
- Full stops, capital letters, question marks and exclamation marks used.
- Fronted adverbials used, but without commas.

Transcription

- Some spelling errors; for example, quikly, cloths, whith, exitment. Further understanding of suffixes needed; for example, -ly (realy), -ed (opend).

Tornado Strikes

One one calm Sunday morning at 08:00AM a tornado struck. Everyone panicked but then Mr Wharton and his mum got sucked into the vast, whirling, swirling, dust splitting tornado and never came out. Still to this day mo-one knows where they are.

A reporter came at 01:00PM and this is Mrs Dye's point of view, "Well it was terrifying I didn't know what was going on." Suddenly a Storm Chaser came in the tornado intercept veichles, this is what he said, "It was an interesting tornado completely unlike the others I've seen."

The rain came and will it ever stop?

Who knows?

Composition

- Simple organisational devices used; for example, heading.
- Factual style with interviews appropriate for a newspaper report.

Grammar and Punctuation

- Headline used as an organisational device.
- Apostrophe used for possession and contracted forms.
- Fronted adverbials used, but without commas.
- Beginnings of rich vocabulary; for example, dust splitting tornado.
- Full stops, capital letters, commas or lists and question marks used.
- Paragraphs organised around a theme.
- Range of determiners used; for example, a, the, this, an.

Transcription

- Spelling mostly correct.

The Tongo Lizard have very sharp claws, they look like shining blades. It's skin is scaly and rough and it's coulor is smoky black. It's fifteen cm high, 45cm long and 20cm width. It's eyes are devil red, they shine I the night and they can see in the dark.

It lives in a rainforest, its wet, gloomy and more wet here. Its house is in the trees it makes a nest out of leaves and stays there. In the rainforest the temperature is 11C.

It eats leaves, plants, insects, small animals and birds. It eats them by hiding in a tree when the pray comes along it jumps out and attacks.

Its endangered because people want it for things like skin, medicane, food and for decoration. Its also because people are chopping down their homes.

Composition

- Paragraphs used to report on different aspects of the topic.
- Informative style appropriate for the audience.
- Rich and varied vocabulary used.

Grammar and Punctuation

- Present perfect form of verbs used (have).
- Sentence with more than one clause.
- Apostrophe only correctly used for contracted forms once; for example, it's.
- Coordination and subordination used; for example, and, because.
- Full stops, capital letters and commas for lists are used.

Transcription

- Some spelling errors; for example, coulor, medicane.

Genre of Samples:

A: Narrative

B: Description of a Scene

C: Diary

D: Newspaper

E: Report

A - Narrative

It was a cloudy afternoon and a small girl named Lizzie was sitting in the soft branches of her silver birch tree.

"Hallo" she wispered to the birds. "Are you okay today?" Chiff and Chaff answered politley "Yes" replied the twins. Suddenly the tree rocked violently. Egglet rolled off the tree an landed with a deafning thump! At the bottom of the tree stood Ghosyie, laughing his head off. Lizzie clambered down the tree. She examined the egg carefully. There was a gigantic crack through the top. When Lizzie went to rest for a nap Bananas and Snowy hooted at the tops of their voices. Magically Wizzling aooeared in a puff of threataning black smoke. With his magic crack was fixed. "Thank you" weezed the baby egg shyly. Postit flew past with a long brown envelope, dropping it in Lizzie's lap.

Dear Liz,

HELP! I'm stuck

Love Dad x

Lizzie dialed a number on her walkey-talkey 875 663. She spoke to him "Hi Dad" "Hi Lizzie" he said. She asked where he was stuck. "I'm stuck in a big ------ unfinished

Anxiously, I edged towards the dark green forest. Below the trees stood a stick-like figure holding what looked like a dead animal. I saw a witch-like dwarf hiding in the trees, she was staring at the creature with its glowing red eyes. The tall, green trees, cut were swaying gently in a blow of the wind where in a deep, blue stream that went right through the forest. The tall, brown stick figure was marching through the deep, blue empty river he walked over to the bright, yellow light in the distance. Although the creature was splashing away, I saw the dwarf in the tree jump into the stream to chase him. Anxiously, I followed them to end my curiosity of them. The light was as bright as the sun, I knew that it was not the sun…

I got to the end of the forest, where were they

Dear Diary

Today I woke up tired and sleepy, but I still got up because it was my birthday! After that I ran past my dad and into the kitchen. Then I eat my breakfast realy quikly, after I eat my breakfast I ran back upstairs to get changed into my birthday cloths and I put my mum's make-up on just don't tell dad ok? Suddenly I heard a realy loud knock on my front door. I called my dad "Dad someone is knocking on the door" Then I slowly opend the door. "Hi Lizzie!" Tommy shouted. Then my dad said "I will bring the birthday cake in the minute" Then I jumped up and down whith exitment while I was blowing out the candles. Then the birthday candles went crazy! Luckly my dad ran in whith a bucket of water and he saved me and tommy.

Today was a dangrose day but a fun day to!

From Lizzie

Tornado Strikes

One one calm Sunday morning at 08:00AM a tornado struck. Everyone panicked but then Mr Wharton and his mum got sucked into the vast, whirling, swirling, dust splitting tornado and never came out. Still to this day mo-one knows where they are.

A reporter came at 01:00PM and this is Mrs Dye's point of view, "Well it was terrifying I didn't know what was going on." Suddenly a Storm Chaser came in the tornado intercept veichles, this is what he said, "It was an interesting tornado completely unlike the others I've seen."

The rain came and will it ever stop?

Who knows?

978-1-84654-883-3   Prim-Ed Publishing   www.prim-ed.com

The Tongo Lizard have very sharp claws, they look like shining blades. It's skin is scaly and rough and it's coulor is smoky black. It's fifteen cm high, 45cm long and 20cm width. It's eyes are devil red, they shine I the night and they can see in the dark.

It lives in a rainforest, its wet, gloomy and more wet here. Its house is in the trees it makes a nest out of leaves and stays there. In the rainforest the temperature is 11C.

It eats leaves, plants, insects, small animals and birds. It eats them by hiding in a tree when the pray comes along it jumps out and attacks.

Its endangered because people want it for things like skin, medicane, food and for decoration. Its also because people are chopping down their homes.

Genre of Samples:

A: Narrative

B: Diary

C: Report

D: Narrative

E: Speech

Stone Age Boy

Through the old, gloomy woods was a figure of a boy. Suddenly, he found himself falling down, down, down. When he woke up he was in a dark plaece. In the distance he saw the light so the figure folloed it. Outside it was a forist again, there were moutines and animals. "H" the boy wisped. He saw figure of a girl, she had ginger hair a, red coat, brown trousers, shoes and a bag.

Now for a little walk the girl toke the boy to her family. The boy heard the girl talking, to one of her family. "Look at this boy." The girl wisped. "Om where did you find him? " The woman replied "He was lost." Om said Around the busy, cold campsite, people were making tools, woluing and sewing clothes. Stone Age Boy felt incredibly tired.

That afternoon the sun shone like a firework. Exploring and excited the little boys and girls happily picked berries and nuts. Wildly the Stone Age people ran to the sea, and fro there spears at the water. A boy was shouting and poiting to a raindear. Everyone screamed frowing the spears some one fron there spear and got thw side of the dear. Now everyone had a sellabrashen Stone Age boy

Composition

- Setting and character introduced in first sentence.
- Paragraphs organised around a theme.
- Rich and varied vocabulary.

Grammar and Punctuation

- Preposition of time used as a story opener.
- Fronted adverbials used, but commas not used consistently.
- Commas in a list mostly used accurately.
- Range of determiners used; for example, a, the, this, that.
- Direct speech used and punctuated.
- Capital letters, full stops, commas and a question mark are used.
- Some sentences with more than one clause, although punctuation within the sentence is missing.

Transcription

- Some spelling errors; for example, plaece, folloed, forist, moutines. toke.

Dear Diary,

Would you like to have a life were you cannot do anything without your dad following you about twenty four seven? No you would not. Well thats the life I have to live it's horrible trust me. Well anyway on this bright and sunny day, which is my birthday I am 10 years old and we went and bought our new bird so the 13 other birds on our tree will have a new freind. Just then, in the blink of an eye, as soon as they met they were freinds. Totally overwhelmed, I ran back to my dad, who had bought me the bird in the first place and he is very excited to know that they were getting along just fine.

But one day, I saw my new lovely beautiful and brown bird hitting and peering at Zara one of my other birds in my tree. I thought to myself "Why are they doing this" one minute there freinds next their not. Maybe they have freind issues or maybe their just messing I'll go and look. When I went outside I thought to myself I want a new bike mabe we could all go on a ride. The birds were ok but their was something not right about this new bird. I called him Harley. We went on our bike ride the birds were flying and I was riding. Then Harley flew infront of me I lost control and crashed. I snapped both my legs and broke one of my ribs. I was severely injured. I had to stay in hospital which quite nice because there was a computer (which was excellent) so I couldn't go on my games.

Composition

- Informal style and questioning the reader appropriate for diary.

Grammar and Punctuation

- Fronted adverbials used.
- Apostrophes used for contractions.
- Sentences extended by using subordinate clauses.
- Present and past perfect forms of verbs used.
- Range of determiners used; for example, this, the, a, an, one.
- Nouns and pronouns suitable for text.
- Direct speech used and punctuated.
- Capital letters, full stops, commas and a question mark used.

Transcription

- Spelling mostly correct, with few errors; for example, freind. The homophone 'there' and 'their' have been used instead of 'they're'.

C - Report

The Tongo Lizard looks like a smooth scaly rat it's about 4.3cm in height and 2.1cm in size. This endangered lizard has pointy, long and spicky sabour tooth teeth. The Tongo Lizard can change its colour but its mostly emerald green, ruby red and daimond blue.

The Tongi Lizard eyes are hazle brown eyes but if you look close there are tiny emerald shards. The Tongo Lizards skin is scaly smooth, shiny, sparkly and blinding. The Tongo Lizards tong is one of the most important part of its body it smashes it prey with a bang and squashes it's prey and sucks it in. The Tongo Lizards tail is long and thick if the creature is being attacks by both directions it uses it's tong and tail. The Tongo Lizard claws are sharp as scissors.

The Tongo Lizard lives in the wide, scorching western fields. There are lots of dangerous, spicky cacti there are few trees whith no leaves on them. The western fields are 70 C very hot scorching weather only small lakes that get evaporated in just 23 hours.

The Tongo lizard is in the middle of the food chain it eats gerbous and digs into juicy cactuses. The Tingo lizard squash there prey with it's tong and tail rarely if it is hungry it may eat other types of lizards. It eats juicy cactus and digs into it.

The Tongo lizard is endangered because it is hunted by cyoties and mountain loins it sometimes dies by trying to eat the juicy cactuses and also poeple like collecting it's teeth and the spike on it's tail help protect the Tongo lizard.

Composition

- Paragraphs used to report on different aspects of the topic.
- Informative style appropriate for the audience.
- Rich and varied vocabulary used.

Grammar and Punctuation

- Preposition used.
- Apostrophe in 'it's' used for contraction.
- Commas used in lists.
- Varied and rich vocabulary; for example, tiny emerald shards.
- Conjunctions used to joins clauses; for example, but, because.

Transcription

- Some spelling errors; for example, sabour, daimond, hazle, tong, poeple.

Lost and Found

"Go and sell some Sugarcane Juice for me. Don't forget two ruppees a glass," orded Abba. As soon as Abba said this Hamid his son was there holding out his hands for a tray of the sweet Sugarcane Juice. When he got onto to the bus because he followed Bulbul the conjurer. "How many times have I told my son to keep away from that silly old conjurer or whatever his name is!" shouted Abba angrily. Everybody looked at Abba shocked. Abba went as red as a tomatoe. After, a while Abba realised that he hadn't seen his son for a while. His son was missing … Abba spotted Hamid on the bus to Timapur. The bus speeds down the street pushing people out of his way. Then the wind blew heavily and knocked down a cart wich got in Abba's way and the person who owend it was very old and couldn't pick it up so Abba had to do it for him. Just, as he finished the bus zoomed past them knocking the cart over once again but cursed Uncle. Abba asked his friends, "Do you know wich way the bus went?" they just shrugged there shoulders as asked why. Abba told them a the hole story a little bear appead in his eye. All his friends offered him free things but he declined determend to find his son. How could he do it though. The bus station smelt smellier than normal, it looked more ugly than normal as well. Was it his son who made it the best place in the world? Abba wasn't going to give up now though but how. Abba thought as hood as a brick glough he was as smart as a witch. All along he was trying to run after a bus when all ne needed to do was get a different bus! It was a very smart plan indeed. He waits for the next bus. When he got onto the bus, he thought he was going to find his son until it took the wrong turn. Finally, Abba gave up and walked back to the bus station. He found his son there and was overwhelmed with himself. He gave his son a great big hug.

Composition
- Characters introduced in the first two sentences.

Grammar and Punctuation
- Direct speech fully punctuated.
- Apostrophes used for possession and contraction.
- Adverbs used throughout writing.
- Capital letters, full stops, commas, exclamation marks and question marks used accurately.
- Sentences have more than one clause.
- Conjunctions used to join clauses.
- Front adverbial used, though not always with correct comma usage.

Transcription
- Some spelling errors; for example, tomatoe, wich, owened, appead. There are some errors with homophones; for example, there/their and hole/whole.

E – Speech

Hey fans of Battle Attack, you should know the all great and powerful. They called me tough, undefeating, no I am not Horrid Horse, Mayhem Monkey or Capturing Cat. I am Battle Bunny, the star of the show. If you plan on eliminating me then I would think twice about your 'evil' scheme.

Last week, I broke the glass slipper of Cinderella so the prince wouldn't find his true love and that's no word of a lie. On Wednesday, I stole the perfect presents from Father Christmas and broke every single toy and then delivered them like a pile of rubbish and that's no word of a lie. Earlier this week, I drained the power of the sun and that is no word of a lie. A few weeks ago, I made Usain Bolt trip up before the finish line and that is know word of a lie. Next year, I am planning to conquer my Evil plan into action by throwing megatron bombs at the Eiffel tower so it will blow up and that is no word of a lie.

When I take over the world, you'll have to bow to the king Battle Bunny. Because I'll be king, you'll be my slaves. Watch your back, I am always closer than you think!

Composition

- Character introduced in first paragraph.
- Paragraphs organised around a theme.

Grammar and Punctuation

- Fronted adverbials used correctly.
- Conjunctions used to join clauses.
- Most sentences accurately demarcated, including the comma after fronted adverbials, the apostrophe and capital letters for proper nouns.

Transcription

- Spelling correct, although the homophone 'know' has been used instead of 'no'.

Genre of Samples:

A: Narrative

B: Diary

C: Report

D: Narrative

E: Speech

Stone Age Boy

Through the old, gloomy woods was a figure of a boy. Suddenly, he found himself falling down, down, down. When he woke up he was in a dark plaece. In the distance he saw the light so the figure folloed it. Outside it was a forist again, there were moutines and animals. "H" the boy wisped. He saw figure of a girl, she had ginger hair a, red coat, brown trousers, shoes and a bag.

Now for a little walk the girl toke the boy to her family. The boy heard the girl talking, to one of her family. "Look at this boy." The girl wisped. "Om where did you find him? " The woman replied "He was lost." Om said Around the busy, cold campsite, people were making tools, woluing and sewing clothes. Stone Age Boy felt incredibly tired.

That afternoon the sun shone like a firework. Exploring and excited the little boys and girls happily picked berries and nuts. Wildly the Stone Age people ran to the sea, and fro there spears at the water. A boy was shouting and poiting to a raindear. Everyone screamed frowing the spears some one fron there spear and got thw side of the dear. Now everyone had a sellabrashen Stone Age boy

Dear Diary,

Would you like to have a life were you cannot do anything without your dad following you about twenty four seven? No you would not. Well thats the life I have to live it's horrible trust me. Well anyway on this bright and sunny day, which is my birthday I am 10 years old and we went and bought our new bird so the 13 other birds on our tree will have a new freind. Just then, in the blink of an eye, as soon as they met they were freinds. Totally overwhelmed, I ran back to my dad, who had bought me the bird in the first place and he is very excited to know that they were getting along just fine.

But one day, I saw my new lovely beautiful and brown bird hitting and peering at Zara one of my other birds in my tree. I thought to myself "Why are they doing this" one minute there freinds next their not. Maybe they have freind issues or maybe their just messing I'll go and look. When I went outside I thought to myself I want a new bike mabe we could all go on a ride. The birds were ok but their was something not right about this new bird. I called him Harley. We went on our bike ride the birds were flying and I was riding. Then Harley flew infront of me I lost control and crashed. I snapped both my legs and broke one of my ribs. I was severely injured. I had to stay in hospital which quite nice because there was a computer (which was excellent) so I couldn't go on my games.

The Tongo Lizard looks like a smooth scaly rat it's about 4.3cm in height and 2.1cm in size. This endangered lizard has pointy, long and spicky sabour tooth teeth. The Tongo Lizard can change its colour but its mostly emerald green, ruby red and daimond blue.

The Tongi Lizard eyes are hazle brown eyes but if you look close there are tiny emerald shards. The Tongo Lizards skin is scaly smooth, shiny, sparkly and blinding. The Tongo Lizards tong is one of the most important part of its body it smashes it prey with a bang and squashes it's prey and sucks it in. The Tongo Lizards tail is long and thick if the creature is being attacks by both directions it uses it's tong and tail. The Tongo Lizard claws are sharp as scissors.

The Tongo Lizard lives in the wide, scorching western fields. There are lots of dangerous, spicky cacti there are few trees whith no leaves on them. The western fields are 70 C very hot scorching weather only small lakes that get evaporated in just 23 hours.

The Tongo lizard is in the middle of the food chain it eats gerbous and digs into juicy cactuses. The Tingo lizard squash there prey with it's tong and tail rarely if it is hungry it may eat other types of lizards. It eats juicy cactus and digs into it.

The Tongo lizard is endangered because it is hunted by cyoties and mountain loins it sometimes dies by trying to eat the juicy cactuses and also poeple like collecting it's teeth and the spike on it's tail help protect the Tongo lizard.

Lost and Found

"Go and sell some Sugarcane Juice for me. Don't forget two ruppees a glass," orded Abba. As soon as Abba said this Hamid his son was there holding out his hands for a tray of the sweet Sugarcane Juice. When he got onto to the bus because he followed Bulbul the conjurer. "How many times have I told my son to keep away from that silly old conjurer or whatever his name is!" shouted Abba angrily. Everybody looked at Abba shocked. Abba went as red as a tomatoe. After, a while Abba realised that he hadn't seen his son for a while. His son was missing … Abba spotted Hamid on the bus to Timapur. The bus speeds down the street pushing people out of his way. Then the wind blew heavily and knocked down a cart wich got in Abba's way and the person who owend it was very old and couldn't pick it up so Abba had to do it for him. Just, as he finished the bus zoomed past them knocking the cart over once again but cursed Uncle. Abba asked his friends, "Do you know wich way the bus went?" they just shrugged there shoulders as asked why. Abba told them a the hole story a little bear appead in his eye. All his friends offered him free things but he declined determend to find his son. How could he do it though. The bus station smelt smellier than normal, it looked more ugly than normal as well. Was it his son who made it the best place in the world? Abba wasn't going to give up now though but how. Abba thought as hood as a brick glough he was as smart as a witch. All along he was trying to run after a bus when all ne needed to do was get a different bus! It was a very smart plan indeed. He waits for the next bus. When he got onto the bus, he thought he was going to find his son until it took the wrong turn. Finally, Abba gave up and walked back to the bus station. He found his son there and was overwhelmed with himself. He gave his son a great big hug.

Hey fans of Battle Attack, you should know the all great and powerful. They called me tough, undefeating, no I am not Horrid Horse, Mayhem Monkey or Capturing Cat. I am Battle Bunny, the star of the show. If you plan on eliminating me then I would think twice about your 'evil' scheme.

Last week, I broke the glass slipper of Cinderella so the prince wouldn't find his true love and that's no word of a lie. On Wednesday, I stole the perfect presents from Father Christmas and broke every single toy and then delivered them like a pile of rubbish and that's no word of a lie. Earlier this week, I drained the power of the sun and that is no word of a lie. A few weeks ago, I made Usain Bolt trip up before the finish line and that is know word of a lie. Next year, I am planning to conquer my Evil plan into action by throwing megatron bombs at the Eiffel tower so it will blow up and that is no word of a lie.

When I take over the world, you'll have to bow to the king Battle Bunny. Because I'll be king, you'll be my slaves. Watch your back, I am always closer than you think!

Genre of Samples:

A: Description

B: Letter

C: Recount – Story

D: Narrative

E: Narrative

This dragon (Electra) may look cute, but she is deadly dangerous when it comes to battle. Even though Electra is pretty small, she can sneak up on you and breath fire and electric bombs. She breathes fire when she is happy, excited and also angry. Oh and I couldn't forget, she breathes electric bombs when she is sad, or sometimes angry. In battle she will use both her powers. Although this dragon may sound great, she is sooooo disobedient …

As soon as you look away … SHE'S OFF! I'm warning you now, if she run's away, DO NOT call her name. this speedy dragon is rappid. If you call her name, she'll turn around, stare at you and then … CARRY ON RUNNING! The only way you can get her back is when she is stood still in a world of her own.

Did I Mention that this dragon is a beautiful sea blue colour. She has twinkling eyes that are moss green. Her scaly wings will swoop you away.

Composition
- Description has narrative and descriptive elements.
- Paragraphs organised around a theme.
- Rich and varied vocabulary used.

Grammar and Punctuation
- Brackets used to give extra information.
- Conjunctions used to join clauses; for example, but.
- Apostrophes used within contractions.
- More advanced adverbs used; for example, still.
- Nouns and pronouns used appropriately.
- Full stops, capital letters and exclamation marks used.
- Sentences with subordinate clauses.
- Conjunctions used for subordination and coordination.
- Rich and varied vocabulary developing; for example, disobedient, twinkling.

Transcription
- Spelling mostly correct with very few errors; for example, rappid.

Dear Son,

As you know, your Mother died when you were one week old and I was heartbroken. I always tried my very best. However I must now tell you something about your past.

When you were an infant, I had a dog called Gelert. He was trustworthy and faithful so I trusted him to protect you. Early one morning, I went hunting and I left Gelert watching over you. When I returned I saw blood on the walls, floor and Gelert's mouth. In blind fury, I snatched my diamond, strange sword and I plunged it into Gelert's loyal heart. Suddenly I heard crying from your position. A moment later I saw a wolf. Instantly I turned around and realised he has saved your life but it was too late. I felt horrified and disgusted. So I gone and buried Gelert under a birch oak tree.

Perhaps you may come round and visit Gelert's brave grave and we can remember our brave loyal dog.

Love From Father

Composition

- Informal style appropriate for personal letter.
- Paragraphs organised around a theme.
- Rich and varied vocabulary used.

Grammar and Punctuation

- Fronted adverbials used, but not always with commas.
- Apostrophe used for possession.
- Adverbs used to show time and cause.
- Commas used in lists.
- Sentences with more than one clause.
- Preposition used to show location.
- Sentences accurately punctuated throughout.
- Tenses not always correct; for example, gone/went.
- Rich and varied vocabulary.

Transcription

- Spelling correct.

C – Recount – Story

Last Sunday, I was walking home from my friends and I saw a group of birds. Somebody spotted a name tag on a bird. It said "Superbird" on the blue and red name tag. Carefully I picked that bird up, it looked like it was injured.

Obviously I took it home to my Grandpa, (he's a vet), he said that he had a broken leg … 2 days later I went back to the tree that I found Superbird in and there was a group of birds looking around. I saw another name tag (purple and black) that had the name Banana written all over it.

With the corner of my eye, I saw a voice simulatoe. I thought it was to make my voice go funny but it wasn't It was a device to make me know what the birds are saying. I listened closely and I could just about say what the birds were saying. Banana was asking "Where is Superbird, Superbird, where are you?" I went up the tree and started cheeping like a bird …

I looked down and my feet and they weren't my normal feet. They were bird feet! I looked in my tiny mirror … "Ahhh, I'm a bird!" I exclaimed.

And that was the last people heard from me and now I'm living in Bird Land!…

Composition
- Character and plot have been developed.
- Paragraphs organised around a theme.

Grammar and Punctuation
- Fronted adverbials used.
- Subordinate clauses mostly correct.
- Direct speech used and correctly punctuated.
- Variety of determiners used; for example, the, a, that.
- Capital letters, full stops, commas, brackets, exclamation marks and a question mark are used correctly.
- Apostrophes used for contractions.
- Nouns and pronouns chosen appropriately.
- Adverbs and propositions used to show time and effect.

Transcription
- Spelling mostly correct with very few errors; for example, simulatoe.

Superbird adventures

One day there was a bird like never before and his name was superbird. He is a superhero. Superbird goes in all sorts of adventures like climbing mount everst and riding dinosaurs but best of all he is the one that actually discovered America. On this epic adventure he will be going to Mars to try and discover alian life. With him will be his best friend in the whole entire tree will be the strongest bird ever, Marvin Muscles. They had been best friends since bird next primary. But to make the rocket they would have to go to that Scrapyard and build a rocket out of metal that has been dumped there by other birds. "Look over there!" screamed Marvin "Theres a rocket engine." "Cool!" yelled Superbird. As they were running to the engine their arch enemy Dr crow swooped in and stole the rocket engine. So with that Superbird and Marvin pelted off after him. So the chase began. Marvin and Superbird had secret powers that made them fly faster, so it was a piece of cake for them to catch up to the sloq crow. But he'd got caught up in a tree so the rocket engine just drifted back to them. "That was easier than I thought."

It took them nearly 6 hours but they got it done. Whith swetting foreheads the great launch began. 5 4 3 2 1 BOOM! They set off like a bullet out of a gun. It them around 50 hours to get their but they made it. "Remember your spacesuit," confirmed Superbird. "Yeah." Marvin responded.

Composition
- Characters and plot have been developed.

Grammar and Punctuation
- Direct speech used and correctly punctuated.
- Conjunctions used to separate clauses.
- Apostrophes used for contraction correctly, another omitted.
- Present perfect form of the verb 'have' used; for example, has, have.
- Variety of determiners used; for example, a, the, this.
- Subordinate clauses used within sentences, but with some punctuation missing.
- Capital letters, full stops and exclamation marks used.
- Nouns and pronouns chosen appropriately.

Transcription
- Some spelling errors; for example, alian, sloq, swetting. There is an error with the homophone their/there.

On one beautifully sunny day, Stan was in the garden and then he had a huge, intelligent brain wave. He would make a rocket and his dream would come true because he could fly into the space.

Stan went into the garden shed and got some white paint, red finds and top and a round piece of glass, but what of his dad notices all the things that have gone, and he needs steal.

"Well I'll just have to ___ wood." he said to himself.

So he got cracking when he was finished he admired his master piece.

The rocket had a bright white body, ruby red fins and top a sparkly, gleaming, siny, crystal clear blue window and last but not least three buttons blue, green and yellow. He was a second away from being the worlds youngest astronaut!

When he climbed into his masterpiece he took a deep breth in and pulled the leaver and shot of into space. As he shot of he felt as if he was in a dream bubble that took him into space. He was that happy that he couldn't stop smiling.

When he landed on the moon he got out of the rocket and it was quite hard to breath. He sat down and it was a very rough and uncomfortable surface, but he sat down and got on with it.

Happily, Stan closed his eyes and relaxed and

Composition

- Setting, character and plot have been well developed.
- Paragraphs organised around a theme.
- Rich and varied vocabulary.

Grammar and Punctuation

- Fronted adverbials used with commas.
- Apostrophes used with contractions.
- Conjunctions used to separate clauses.
- Rich and varied vocabulary; for example, gleaming, masterpiece.
- Adverbs and prepositions used to show time and effect.
- Direct speech used and correctly punctuated.
- Nouns and pronouns chosen appropriately.

Transcription

- Some spelling errors; for example, siny, breth, leaver, of.

when he opened his eyes he looked at the twinkling stars. Then a big, green shape passed by like a cheetah.

"Great Scot!" said Stan. "Was that a shooting star?"

Whatever it was it landed next to Stan and he realised it was a spaceship! Then a blue creature crawled out!

Stan was scared then he realised it was friendly and slimy, but he couldn't keep it as a pet because it was an alien.

Genre of Samples:

A: Description

B: Letter

C: Recount – Story

D: Narrative

E: Narrative

This dragon (Electra) may look cute, but she is deadly dangerous when it comes to battle. Even though Electra is pretty small, she can sneak up on you and breath fire and electric bombs. She breathes fire when she is happy, excited and also angry. Oh and I couldn't forget, she breathes electric bombs when she is sad, or sometimes angry. In battle she will use both her powers. Although this dragon may sound great, she is sooooo disobedient …

As soon as you look away … SHE'S OFF! I'm warning you now, if she run's away, DO NOT call her name. this speedy dragon is rappid. If you call her name, she'll turn around, stare at you and then … CARRY ON RUNNING! The only way you can get her back is when she is stood still in a world of her own.

Did I Mention that this dragon is a beautiful sea blue colour. She has twinkling eyes that are moss green. Her scaly wings will swoop you away.

Dear Son,

As you know, your Mother died when you were one week old and I was heartbroken. I always tried my very best. However I must now tell you something about your past.

When you were an infant, I had a dog called Gelert. He was trustworthy and faithful so I trusted him to protect you. Early one morning, I went hunting and I left Gelert watching over you. When I returned I saw blood on the walls, floor and Gelert's mouth. In blind fury, I snatched my diamond, strange sword and I plunged it into Gelert's loyal heart. Suddenly I heard crying from your position. A moment later I saw a wolf. Instantly I turned around and realised he has saved your life but it was too late. I felt horrified and disgusted. So I gone and buried Gelert under a birch oak tree.

Perhaps you may come round and visit Gelert's brave grave and we can remember our brave loyal dog.

Love From Father

Last Sunday, I was walking home from my friends and I saw a group of birds. Somebody spotted a name tag on a bird. It said "Superbird" on the blue and red name tag. Carefully I picked that bird up, it looked like it was injured.

Obviously I took it home to my Grandpa, (he's a vet), he said that he had a broken leg … 2 days later I went back to the tree that I found Superbird in and there was a group of birds looking around. I saw another name tag (purple and black) that had the name Banana written all over it.

With the corner of my eye, I saw a voice simulatoe. I thought it was to make my voice go funny but it wasn't It was a device to make me know what the birds are saying. I listened closely and I could just about say what the birds were saying. Banana was asking "Where is Superbird, Superbird, where are you?" I went up the tree and started cheeping like a bird …

I looked down and my feet and they weren't my normal feet. They were bird feet! I looked in my tiny mirror … "Ahhh, I'm a bird!" I exclaimed.

And that was the last people heard from me and now I'm living in Bird Land!...

Superbird adventures

One day there was a bird like never before and his name was superbird. He is a superhero. Superbird goes in all sorts of adventures like climbing mount everst and riding dinosaurs but best of all he is the one that actually discovered America. On this epic adventure he will be going to Mars to try and discover alian life. With him will be his best friend in the whole entire tree will be the strongest bird ever, Marvin Muscles. They had been best friends since bird next primary. But to make the rocket they would have to go to that Scrapyard and build a rocket out of metal that has been dumped there by other birds. "Look over there!" screamed Marvin "Theres a rocket engine." "Cool!" yelled Superbird. As they were running to the engine their arch enemy Dr crow swooped in and stole the rocket engine. So with that Superbird and Marvin pelted off after him. So the chase began. Marvin and Superbird had secret powers that made them fly faster, so it was a piece of cake for them to catch up to the sloq crow. But he'd got caught up in a tree so the rocket engine just drifted back to them. "That was easier than I thought."

It took them nearly 6 hours but they got it done. Whith swetting foreheads the great launch began. 5 4 3 2 1 BOOM! They set off like a bullet out of a gun. It them around 50 hours to get their but they made it. "Remember your spacesuit," confirmed Superbird. "Yeah." Marvin responded.

On one beautifully sunny day, Stan was in the garden and then he had a huge, intelligent brain wave. He would make a rocket and his dream would come true because he could fly into the space.

Stan went into the garden shed and got some white paint, red finds and top and a round piece of glass, but what of his dad notices all the things that have gone, and he needs steal.

"Well I'll just have to ___ wood." he said to himself.

So he got cracking when he was finished he admired his master piece.

The rocket had a bright white body, a ruby red fins and top a sparkly, gleaming, siny, crystal clear blue window and last but not least three buttons blue, green and yellow. He was a second away from being the worlds youngest astronaut!

When he climbed into his masterpiece he took a deep breth in and pulled the leaver and shot of into space. As he shot of he felt as if he was in a dream bubble that took him into space. He was that happy that he couldn't stop smiling.

When he landed on the moon he got out of the rocket and it was quite hard to breath. He sat down and it was a very rough and uncomfortable surface, but he sat down and got on with it.

Happily, Stan closed his eyes and relaxed and

This artwork was used to inspire some of the 'Lizzie' writing that is included in the collection of writing.

Lizzie loved the silver birch tree in her garden. She would spend hours perched high up in its branches, chatting with the birds who nested there.

Illustration by Mick Robertson
itjustdawnedonme@ntlworld.com

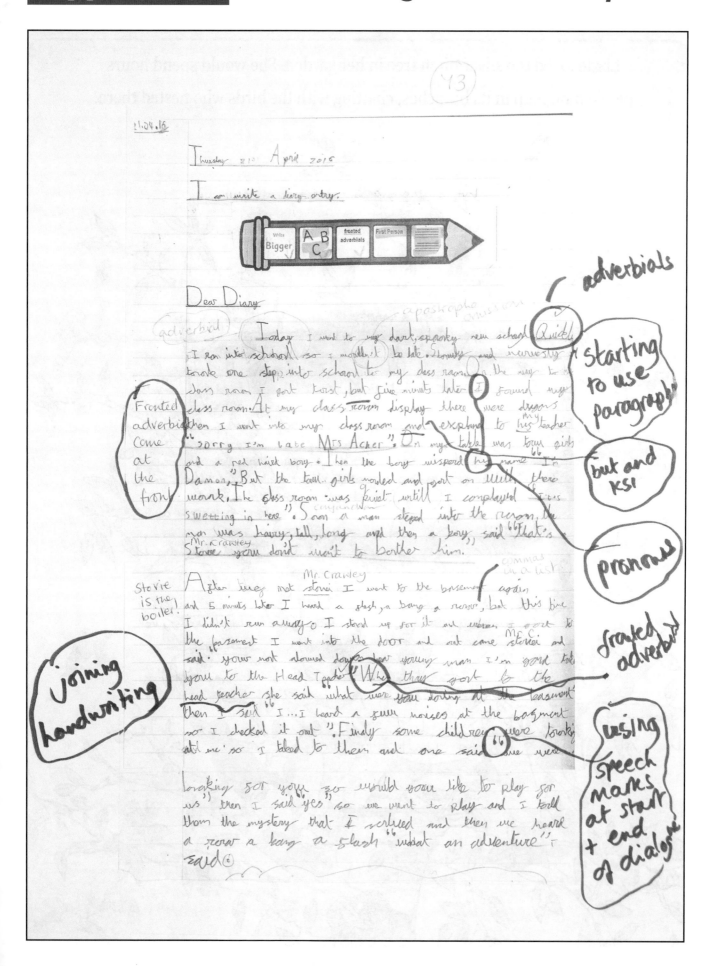

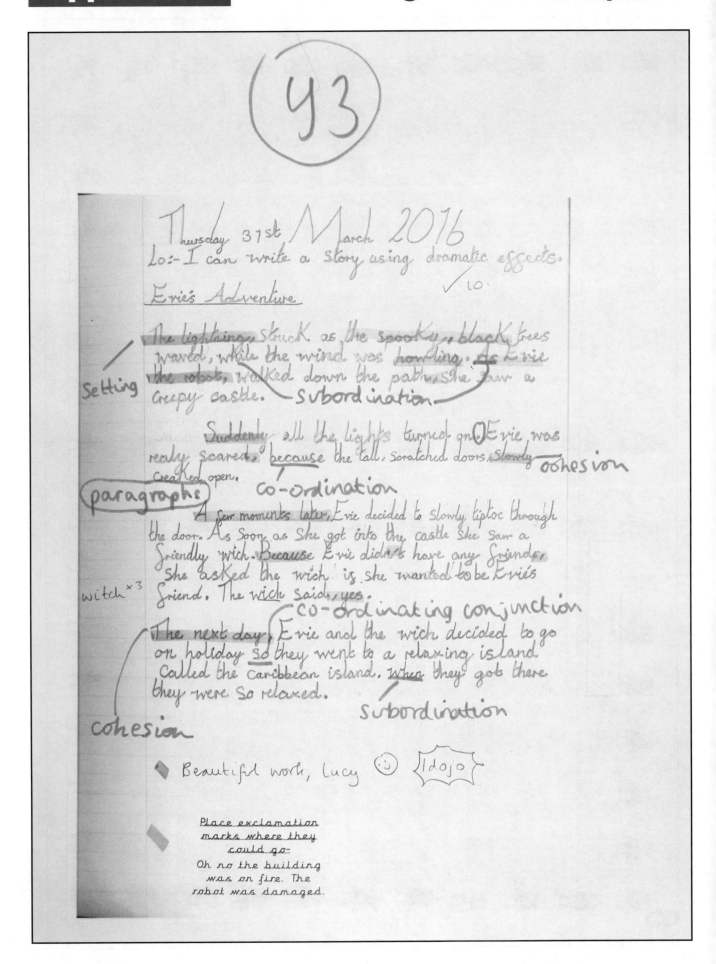

43

Thursday 31st March 2016
Lo:- I can write a story using dramatic effects.
✓ 10.

Evie's Adventure

Setting — The lightning struck as the spooky, black trees waved, while the wind was howling. As Evie the robot, walked down the path, she saw a creepy castle. — *Subordination*

Suddenly all the lights turned on. Evie was really scared, because the tall, scratched doors, slowly — *cohesion* creaked open. — *co-ordination*

paragraphs

A few moments later, Evie decided to slowly tiptoe through the door. As soon as she got into the castle she saw a friendly witch. Because Evie didn't have any friends, she asked the witch if she wanted to be Evie's friend. The witch said, yes.

witch ×3

— *co-ordinating conjunction*

The next day, Evie and the witch decided to go on holiday so they went to a relaxing island called the caribbean island. When they got there they were so relaxed. — *Subordination*

cohesion

◆ Beautiful work, Lucy ☺ [Idojo]

◆ Place exclamation marks where they could go-
Oh no the building was on fire. The robot was damaged.

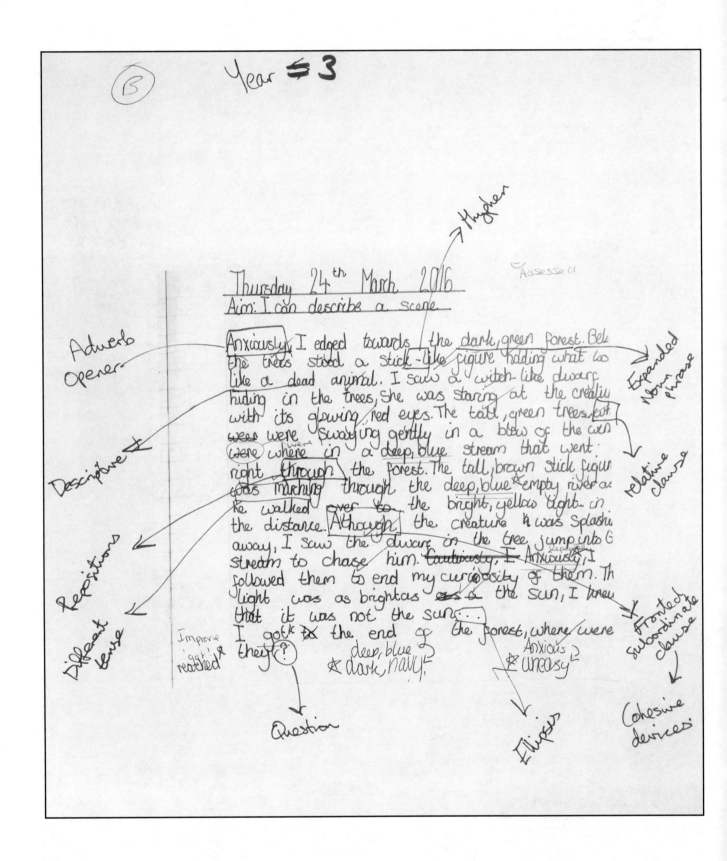

Ⓑ

Year ≤ 3

→ Higher

Assessed

Thursday 24th March 2016
Aim: I can describe a scene.

Adverb Opener →

Anxiously, I edged towards the dark, green forest. Below the trees stood a stick-like figure holding what look like a dead animal. I saw a witch-like dwarf hiding in the trees, she was staring at the creature with its glowing, red eyes. The tall, green trees, were were swaying gently in a blow of the wen were where in a deep, blue stream that went right through the forest. The tall, brown stick figure was marching through the deep, blue empty river as he walked over to the bright, yellow light in the distance. Although the creature it was splashing away, I saw the dwarf in the tree jump into the stream to chase him. Cautiously, I Anxiously, I followed them to end my curiosity of them. The light was as bright as as a the sun, I knew that it was not the sun... I got to the end of the forest, where were they?

Descriptive

Repetitions ↙

Different tense ↙

Improve 'got' → reached

deep, blue ☆ dark, navy.

Anxious ② ☆ uneasy ②

→ Expanded noun phrase

→ Relative clause

↓ Fronted subordinate clause

↓ Cohesive devices

Question ↙

Ellipses ↙

25th February 20

Dear Diary,

(P) 1. Would you like to have a life were you cannot do anything without your ~~dad~~ dad following you about twenty four seven. No you would not. Well thats the life I have to live it's horrible trust me. Well any way on this bright and sunny day, which is my birthday I a 10 years old We went and bought (our) new bird So the 13 other birds on our tree will have new freind. Just then, in the blink of an eye, as soon as they met they were ~~already~~ freind Totally overwhelmed, I ran back to my dad, who b bought me the bird in the first place and he w very excited to know that they were getting alon Just fine.

possessive pronoun

(P) 2. But one day, I saw (my) new ~~new~~ lovely beautiful and brown bird hitting and peeking at Zara one of my other birds on my tree. I thought to myself "why o they doing this one minute there freinds next the not. Maybe they have freind issues or maybe their Just messing I'll go and look. When I went outside I thought to myself I want a new bike mabe we could all go on a ride. The birds were ok but their was some thing not right about this new bird. I called him harley. We went on our bike rid the birds were flying and I was riding. then Harley flew infront of me I lost control and crashed. I snapped both my legs and broke one of my ribs. I w severly injured. I had to stay in hospit which quite nice because there was a compute (which was excellent) So I could go on my games

Annotations (teacher):

- Increasing range of sentence structures
- Question to engage the reader.
- Contraction- apostrophe.
- possessive pronoun.
- Fronted adverbial
- Pronouns for cohesion
- Beginning to use conventions of speech, but not correctly punctuated.
- adverb
- relative clause
- Co-ordinating Conjunction
- Parenthesis

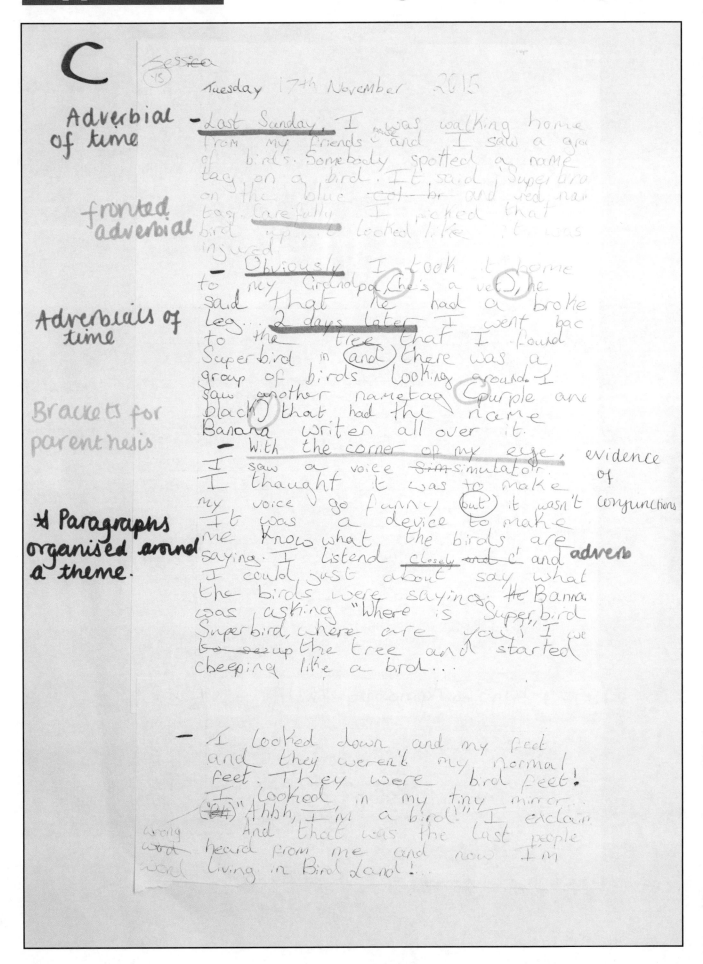

C

Jessica
(YS)

Tuesday 17th November 2015

Adverbial of time — Last Sunday, I was walking home from my friends' and I saw a group of birds. Somebody spotted a name tag on a bird. It said "Superbird" on the blue cot br and red nai tag.

fronted adverbial — Carefully I picked that bird up, it looked like it was injured.

— Obviously I took it home to my Grandpa (he's a vet), he said that he had a broke leg... **Adverbials of time** 2 days later I went bac to the tree that I found Superbird in (and) there was a group of birds looking around. I saw another nametag (purple and **Brackets for parenthesis** black) that had the name Banana writen all over it.

— With the corner of my eye, evidence of I saw a voice sim simulator. conjunctions I thought it was to make my voice go funny (but) it wasn't. **✱ Paragraphs organised around a theme.** It was a device to make me know what the birds are adverb saying. I listend closely and I and I could just about say what the birds were saying. the Banna was asking "Where is Superbird Superbird, where are you!" I we to see up the tree and started cheeping like a bird...

— I looked down and my feet and they weren't my normal feet. They were bird feet! I looked in my tiny mirror... wrong "Ahhh, I'm a bird!" I exclain word And that was the last people word heard from me and now I'm word living in Bird Land!...

Teacher's Moderation Toolkit – Years 3 and 4 978-1-84654-883-3   Prim-Ed Publishing   www.prim-ed.com